6.15

BATS

BATS

BY VALERIE PITT

◄─ A FIRST BOOK ─►

FRANKLIN WATTS
NEW YORK | LONDON | 1976

Frontispiece:
a rare albino bat in flight.

Photographs courtesy of: Sdeuard C. Bisserot, F.R.P.S.: frontispiece, pages 3, 10, 20, 31, 32, 37; National Park Service: pages 14, 25; Zoological Society of London: page 16; New York Zoological Society: pages 24, 40, 45, 53; Interior — U.S. Fish and Wildlife Service: page 43; Cherrie D. Bramwell, photo by David Cole: page 56.

Library of Congress Cataloging in Publication Data

Pitt, Valerie.
    Bats

    (A First book)
    Bibliography: p.
    Includes index.
    SUMMARY: Discusses the physical characteristics and habits of and the myths and superstitions about bats.
    1. Bats — Juvenile literature. [1. Bats] I. Title.
QL737.C5P6   599'.4   76-12535
ISBN 0–531–00335–3

CONTENTS

ACKNOWLEDGMENTS

The author would like to express her warmest thanks to Dr. Paul A. Racey of the Department of Zoology, University of Aberdeen, Scotland, for reading the manuscript of this book and for his helpful suggestions and encouragement. Grateful thanks are also due to the Earl of Cranbrook for sharing firsthand research on his bats-in-hair experiments, and to Dr. Michael Brambell, Curator of Mammals, London Zoo, for his patience and help.

For D.W.

REAL-LIFE DEVILS?

To many people, bats seem to be the most frightening creatures in the whole animal world. Just the sight of one fluttering in the sky at dusk, or flapping its leathery wings behind glass in a zoo, is often enough to cause shrieks of horror.

And if a bat actually gets into a house, then the sort of panic generally reserved for fires and earthquakes often takes hold. Some members of the family may escape hysterically into other rooms. Some may cover themselves with tablecloths or blankets, then lie shuddering underneath. Others may grab weapons — tennis rackets, brooms, baseball bats — almost anything at hand will do. Once combat has begun, it usually ends in death — for the bat, that is. Few people think of simply opening a window to let the creature escape.

Other animals are usually treated more kindly. Wounded birds are bandaged with homemade splints and fed patiently from an eyedropper. A cat, trapped in the topmost branches of a tree, may even have the local fire department called out to rescue it.

Why, then, do bats cause such fear and frenzy during their chance encounters with human beings?

Well, first, there is the question of looks. At first glance

(1)

some bats appear to be downright ugly. And ugly animals often make people feel afraid. Bats' bodies are mouselike. Their faces are often wrinkled and strange-looking. Their claws are grasping, their ears are often pointed like horns, and some have long dangling tails. To top it all, bats have startling cloaklike wings that can suddenly unfold and spread like a parachute. When you consider that the largest *species*, or kinds, may measure nearly 6 feet from wing tip to wing tip, it is not really surprising that to many people bats look like real-life devils. Few people take the trouble to look again and discover their more appealing features. Bats have soft, often beautiful fur, bright little eyes, and perky, almost human expressions. They can also swing and somersault like acrobats.

Bats are *nocturnal* animals — creatures of the night. They spend their waking lives during the hours of darkness when most human beings are sleeping. As the light begins to fade at dusk, flocks of bats, occasionally numbering in the millions, stream out of caves and barns and trees and buildings to begin their hunt for food. At sunrise the last stragglers return to their roosts to sleep away the hours of daylight.

This astonishing ability to find their way and their food in what may be total blackness, also helps give bats their frightening reputation. For, since the earliest times, people have associated darkness with mystery and evil. The traditional hour of ghosts

The extremely large ears of this bat make it a funny-looking creature. Not surprisingly, it is called a long-eared bat.

and goblins, witches and werewolves has always been the dark dead of night. Thus, living in the world of darkness, bats have become objects of countless myths and superstitions.

Folktales and other legends about bats were handed down through the centuries. At best, bats came to be considered as bad omens. And at the worst, they were thought to bring disaster and madness. In 1332 one unfortunate French woman was burned to death at the stake simply because superstitious neighbors complained that her house and walled-in garden attracted crowds of bats.

But there is another reason why many people still regard bats with fear. The famous *vampire bats* of South America live on a diet of blood. While vampires usually bite cattle and horses in order to drink a small quantity of their blood, they sometimes bite human beings too. Although a bat's bite is not dangerous in itself, many vampires carry *rabies* — a serious and usually fatal disease. They can spread the disease to humans and other animals as they feed. Vampires are the only bats that feed on blood, but they give all bat species a bad name.

There are many spine-chilling stories about vampires, but most of them can be traced to works of fiction, and to one work in particular — the horror story *Dracula*. When the Irish author Bram Stoker wrote *Dracula* in 1897, he tried to make it seem realistic. He succeeded so well that many people around the world still think *Dracula* is a true story.

In his novel, Bram Stoker created a vampire that was both human and animal. The name he gave to this creature was Count Dracula. In the story, Count Dracula leaves his eerie castle in the mist-covered mountains of Romania and journeys to England to try to set up a new kingdom of vampires. During the hours from sunrise to sunset the count lies still as death in a coffin. As night falls, he rises — usually in the form of a bat — to dine. Biting the throats of his victims with sharp, white teeth, he sucks their blood until they die and become vampires themselves.

In our own time many horror films, books, and comics have grown up around this story. And lately the fever has spread to other fields. Travel agencies offer a "Dracula tour" of Romania, while one of England's most popular ice creams goes by the name of "Count Dracula's Secret." It has a coating of black water ice and a center filled with "blood-red" jelly.

But while superstitions and spooky stories about bats are good for a shivery laugh, the real truth about these unusual animals is actually much more surprising.

WHAT ARE BATS?

Bats live almost everywhere in the world. They are found in tropical rain forests and on the fringes of deserts, in woods, along seashores, in bush country, in gardens and fields, and even in big cities like New York and London. The only areas where bats do not live are the freezing Arctic and Antarctic regions where food is almost impossible to find.

There are more than one thousand different species of bats, and they are tremendously varied. Some are no bigger than hummingbirds. But some have a wingspan of 2½ feet and look almost as big as rabbits or puppies. The very largest species may have a wingspan of almost 6 feet. They look like flying saucers as they circle the air.

Bats vary in color, too. While most are brown, some species are reddish orange, some are yellow, some are gray, and some are even frosted with silver hairs.

Bats also live on different diets. Most species feed on insects. But there are some others that eat fruit, a few kinds that eat fish, and a few that drink blood. There are even a few that eat small lizards and birds and sometimes each other as well.

Despite these differences, there is one thing that all bat species have in common. They are all **mammals.** Along with tigers and elephants, mice, human beings, bats belong to the large class of animals that suckle (feed) their young with milk.

The word mammal comes from the Latin word *mammae,* meaning "breasts." The females' ability to feed their young with milk from the nipples on their breasts gives mammals their name. It also separates them from all the other main classes of animals — birds, reptiles, insects, and fish. None of these animals is able to produce a single drop of milk.

Mammals have another characteristic in common, too. They all have some hair or fur to keep them warm. The soft fur that covers bats' heads, backs, and bellies traps their body heat and prevents it from drifting off into the cool night air around them.

While bats suckle their young and have furry coats like other mammals, they also have one characteristic that makes them unique. They are the only mammals that have developed wings. This means they are the only mammals capable of true flight. Some exotic kinds of squirrels and a few other rare animals have folds of skin along the sides of their bodies that spread out and allow them to glide from tree to tree for 150 feet or more. But bats are the only mammals that can fly as birds do.

All the mammals have evolved from animals that originally lived on land. And today most mammals still stay fairly close to the ground. No one knows when bats first took to the air. In fact, no one really knows how they evolved or who their direct ancestors were. They are thought to have descended from small tree-dwelling shrews that fed on insects at night. Scientists study **fossils** (the hardened remains of animals preserved in rock) to learn how animals evolved. But so far no fossils of these "missing link" creatures have been found.

However, we do know that bats number among the earliest of today's modern mammals. One almost complete fossil of a bat found in Wyoming dates back some sixty million years. It proves that bats had almost reached their present form at a time when the early ancestors of humans had not yet reached the size of monkeys.

We also know the answer to a mystery that has puzzled people for centuries — the real reason why bats fly only at night. Scientists believe that bats evolved to take advantage of a food supply that had not yet been tapped by any other animal. That food supply was an abundance of night-flying insects.

Insects make up the diet of most bats and most birds. We know from fossils that birds appeared on earth long before bats. Birds evolved from reptiles that searched for food during the daytime hours. Today most kinds of birds also hunt and feed during the day like their early ancestors. Yet not all insects come out during the day — many emerge only at night. Thus, there was also a ready-made food supply for another kind of animal. There was a place for an animal that could both fly and find food in the dark. Evolving as it almost surely did from a nocturnal insect-eater, in time the bat became perfectly adapted for this nighttime role.

HAND-WINGS FOR FLYING

It is their wings that set bats apart from all other mammals. Scientists have divided mammals into eighteen different groups, or *orders*. Because bats are the only mammals that can fly, they are placed in a scientific order of their own. This order is known as Chiroptera (pronounced Kir-op-tera).

Chiroptera comes from two Greek words, *cheir*, meaning "hand," and *pteron*, meaning "wing." "Hand-wings" is a good name, for if you look at a bat's wings, you will see they are rather like human hands — only much more exaggerated in shape. The thumb is short, but the four finger bones are extremely long. The skin is stretched out between them like the webbing between a duck's toes.

Though birds and bats both fly, their wings are constructed quite differently. Birds have feathered wings that are supported by bones along the top edge only. Bats have leathery wings, made up of a double layer of thin skin, or *membrane*. If you look at the picture on the next page, you will see that a bat's arm bones and finger bones spread out to support the entire surface of the wings. Then the wing membranes join up with the bones of the leg for extra support.

Many kinds of bats also have a membrane that stretches between their legs. It can be tucked up to form a pouch that is useful both for catching insects and during the birth of baby bats. And all bats have tools for grasping branches and other perches: their clawed thumbs and toes.

While birds' wings are made up of feathers and bats' wings are made up of skin and bone, the real job of flying is carried out in both cases by powerful chest and shoulder muscles. These muscles respond to nerve impulses sent out from the brain. Bats are not such strong fliers as birds, but they are still able to travel over long distances. And because they have wings like hands, they can flex their knuckles and change the shape of their wings for easy takeoffs, landings, banks, dives, and turns. Small bats can fly with an agility that many birds cannot match. They can dodge

A bat's arm and finger bones support its wing membrane.

through closely spaced lines of thin wire, or between the legs of chairs. Some bats can even fly and turn smoothly inside a cage just three times longer than themselves.

Bats' wings have another useful purpose, too. When bats are resting, the long finger bones close up like the spokes of an umbrella and their wings fold around their bodies. Instead of falling into large, loose folds that could be easily torn on jagged rocks or branches, the wings fall into hundreds of tiny individual folds. The folds form a smooth, snug cloak to help keep out wind and cold. Bats often tuck their heads completely inside their wings when they are sleeping.

KINDS OF BATS

Bats emerge only at night and are not seen as often as more familiar mammals like cats, dogs, and horses. For this reason bats are sometimes thought to make up only a small and unimportant group among the eighteen orders of mammals. In fact, Chiroptera is the second-largest order of mammals. Bats are outnumbered only by rodents.

The one thousand or so species of bats are placed in two suborders for easier identification. These suborders are the Megachiroptera, meaning large bats, and the Microchiroptera, meaning small bats.

Megas are found only in the warmest parts of Africa, Australia, and Asia. They include the very largest bats of all. Known as *flying foxes*, these bats sometimes have a wingspan of nearly 6 feet. Despite their size, Megas are sometimes kept as pets and often make amusing companions. You can read more about bats in captivity later in this book.

The bats we are most familiar with, and the vast majority of species, belong to the suborder Microchiroptera. Micros span the globe and are the most varied bats. They have different habits, different diets, and different ways of life. But they all have unusual looks. Some have ears like pixies, some have grooved and twisted mouths, some have noses shaped like spears. Yet strange as the Micros appear, there is a very practical reason for their looks. They are special adaptations for the unusual lives they lead.

THE EXTRAORDINARY MICROS

ROOSTS

The lives of bats, like those of most other animals, revolve around a homesite, or *roost*. The roost is a sheltered place where they can sleep safely away from enemies after their nightly hunting trips, and digest their food. When the breeding season comes, they bear their young there. Though some kinds of Micros live alone, most species live in colonies with others of their kind. A bat colony may contain dozens of bats, hundreds of bats, thousands of bats, or even millions and millions of bats.

Many Micros choose caves as roosts. Often the caves and tunnels extend deep down into the earth for hundreds of feet. Here where there is no light at all, enormous colonies of bats may make their home, clinging to the roofs and walls in vast, furry clusters.

Carlsbad Caverns in New Mexico usually has a summer population of some ten million bats. Bracken Cave, in Texas, is thought to house a staggering forty million bats during the summer months. As the shrill, squeaking clusters of bats leave Bracken Cave at dusk, they spiral high into the air. Then they disperse in a flock that may measure 20 miles in diameter.

(13)

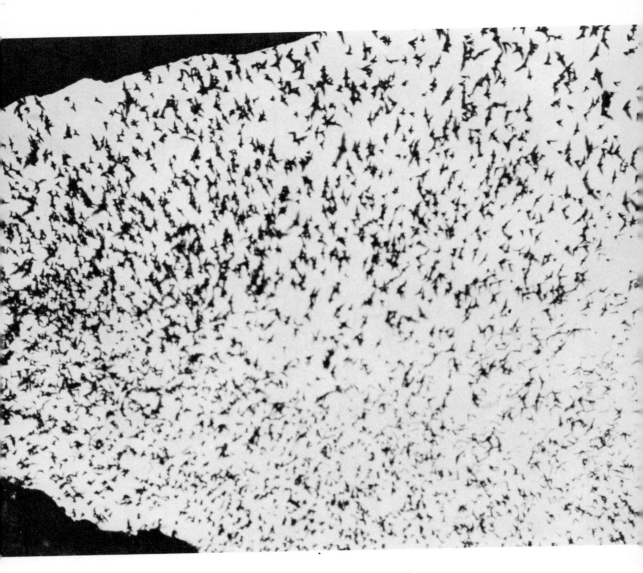

At dusk in the summertime, vast numbers of
bats leave Carlsbad Caverns in New Mexico.

While caves are the best-known roosting sites of bats, some species of Micros choose other kinds of homes. They roost in trees, ruins, mines, tunnels, deep pits, quarries, or the cracks of rocks. Many Micros roost in the rafters of churches, barns, and houses. Some even make their homes in the tombs of Egypt's great pyramids.

Once housed, bats can be quite difficult to remove. And they tend to show decided preferences for certain buildings, returning to them year after year, ignoring other suitable roosts along the way.

While bats do not make nests, a couple of South American species do carve out special homes in palm trees. They cut holes in large palm fronds with their teeth so the leaves bend down at an angle. These tentlike homes provide shelter during heavy rainfalls and periods of glaring heat.

HANGING UPSIDE DOWN

Whatever kinds of homes they choose, all bats spend the time in their roosts hanging upside down by their toes. They have to, for their forelimbs have become so completely adapted for flight that only their short thumbs protrude from their wings. It is much easier to hang from ten strong toes than from two short thumbs.

Bats' toes have very curved, sharp claws. These allow them to get a firm grip on branches, rafters, or the rocky ceilings of caves, and to hang securely for many hours. Even dead bats may be seen still hanging upside down from a perch. Some species of Micros also have suction pads on the soles of their feet, and sometimes on their thumbs as well. These help them to cling to shiny leaves and other smooth surfaces.

Bats' legs have become adapted in order to hold the weight of their bodies as they hang. Their legs are attached to their hip joints in a way opposite to that of other mammals. This means that the knees of most species bend backward, instead of forward as ours do, and the soles of their feet face forward. In a few species, especially the vampires, the knees are turned only sideways. These bats can move about on the ground. They use not only their hind feet but also their wrist joints for added support as they hop about.

When they are resting in their roosts, bats only turn the right way up to pass waste materials. In this way they do not soil their fur. With quick, acrobatic movements, they grasp their perches with their thumbs and let their bodies dangle down. Then they swing their feet up and flip upside down again.

LONG-DISTANCE TRAVELING

Micros of temperate regions do not usually stay put in one roost. Colonies often have several homes within the same general area which they visit when they are feeding in the neighborhood. When the seasons change, they usually **migrate** — travel to a different area entirely. The movements of most North American and European bats follow regular yearly patterns that are cued by changes in the seasons.

This bright-eyed fruit bat seems to be smiling for the camera as it hangs upside down from ten sturdy toes.

A new cycle begins each year in late fall. Then, as the days get colder and food supplies dwindle, all bats face a struggle for survival. Some species cope with the threat of starvation by finding a suitable roost and **hibernating** (sleeping) until the cold weather is over. Other species solve the problem by migrating hundreds of miles to warmer areas where insect food is still available.

It was not until the last century that people became aware that some kinds of bats migrate. Then, in the 1880s, observers noticed that certain American species had changed their range. In summer the *red bat,* the *hoary bat,* and the *silver-haired bat,* were found only north of New York State. In winter they were discovered as far south as Georgia and Texas. The only way the bats could have reached the south was by flying there.

Migrating bats often travel with vast flocks of migrating birds, keeping to well-defined routes along coastlines and mountain ranges. Not all survive the trip. Like many birds, they become confused on foggy nights and crash into lighthouses, tall buildings, and beacons around airports.

Many bats do migrate successfully over long distances though. We know this from bat-ringing experiments. Scientists capture bats, place small metal rings around their forearms, and then release them. When the bats are captured again, it is easy to tell how far they have traveled. When bat-ringing experiments first began, in the 1930s, one bat released in Dresden, Germany, was recovered during the first summer 475 miles away in Lithuania. And in America, bats released in Vermont were found to have traveled around 170 miles to winter quarters in Connecticut. Later banding programs have shown that *free-tailed bats* ringed at

Carlsbad Caverns, New Mexico, migrated over 800 miles south to central Mexico. And that a Balkan species traveled 1,000 miles to its summer home in Russia.

How do bats find their way on these long journeys? Although no one knows for certain, it is believed they rely on vision to memorize major landmarks. They are probably also guided by changing winds and the pattern of the moon and stars. **Instinct,** or inborn knowledge, must also play a part.

STRETCHING FAT RESERVES

Bats that cope with cold weather and lack of food by hibernating usually choose caves as their retreats. Often they use the same caves year after year and may travel many miles to reach them. Once safely inside, the bats huddle together in clusters and fall into a deep torpor, or sleep.

During the next few months the bats must live upon reserves of fat they have built up during the summer when insect food was plentiful. The success of their hibernation will depend on how long they can make their fat reserves last. Bats, and other animals that hibernate, can only conserve fat by conserving energy. To this end, a bat's body **metabolism** slows down. (The rate at which an animal's body uses energy is determined by its metabolism.) As it sinks into deep sleep, a bat's body temperature falls sharply, usually to within one degree of the air temperature around it. Its heartbeats slow dramatically, and it barely breathes at all.

For bats, successful hibernation also depends on how skillfully they choose a hibernation site in the first place. Bats conserve energy best when their body temperatures fall below 50° Fahren-

heit. The most suitable caves have an air temperature ranging between 34° and 50° Fahrenheit. This ideal temperature range is quite narrow, and the lower end is close to the freezing point. If a bat's body temperature falls below freezing, it will not survive for long.

Bats may remain in a state of torpor for as long as five or six months, waking only now and then to drink or make short feeding flights on the warmest nights. Because their body metabolism is so slowed down, hibernation can be a dangerous time for bats. If they are suddenly disturbed by people or by *carnivores* (meat eaters), such as wild cats, it may take five minutes or more for their bodies to warm up enough for them to be able to fly away and escape.

Even when they are not hibernating, bats usually have a slower body metabolism than other mammals. Bats may sleep in their roosts for as long as twenty hours a day, and as they sleep, their temperature falls. This allows them to live much longer than other mammals about their size, such as mice and shrews. Mice and shrews maintain high body temperature all the time and seldom live for longer than a year or two. Because bats have a much lower rate of metabolism for most of the time, and so conserve energy more successfully, they usually live for twelve to fifteen years. Some bats have lived for more than twenty years.

The greater horseshoe bat is a European species that spends the winter hibernating in caves.

STORING SPERM

In spring, around mid-April, bats that have migrated fly back to their old homes. And bats that have relied on fat reserves to keep them alive during the cold winter months come out of hibernation. Soon reproduction will begin. The young will be born in midsummer when an abundance of insects will be there for the catching.

Both male and female bats may mate with many different partners each year. Then the females raise the baby bats alone. Reproduction is not left to chance, however. One remarkable adaptation has been discovered in hibernating species, and it sets these bats apart from all other mammals. Bats that hibernate often mate in the fall before they go into a state of torpor. Astonishingly, the **sperm** the female receives from a male during mating stays alive in her reproductive tract until spring, five or six months later. The sperm of all other male mammals, including human beings, has an active life of a few days at most.

This extraordinary adaptation came to light one winter several years ago when some American biologists collected a number of hibernating bats from caves. While examining the bats, they noticed the females had large numbers of live sperm in their reproductive tracts. At the same time, they noticed something that seemed inconsistent with this fact. The females had not yet released an **egg cell** from one of their ovaries. This process is called **ovulation.** For most mammals, mating must take place very close to the time of ovulation in order for young to be conceived.

Female mammals usually ovulate either once a month or several times a year. But the biologists discovered that bat species that hibernate usually ovulate only *once* a year, in the spring.

Since there are only a couple of days in the entire year when a female bat is able to conceive, then mating cannot be left to chance. The unusually long life of bat sperm is nature's way of ensuring the survival of the species. The perfect way to make sure that a female will conceive is for sperm to be already present at the time of ovulation. In this way the egg can be speedily fertilized. The mother goes through the periods of pregnancy and nursing while there is ample food around. The young are born when food supplies are still plentiful. This gives them time to feed and store up fat before the cold winter months arrive.

A READY-MADE SAFETY NET

Most female bats give birth to one baby each year. Twins are rare, except among the red bats of North America. Pregnancy lasts for around eight weeks in most small species of Micros. By the height of the feeding season, in June and July, many roosts are serving as nursery chambers. They are filled with hundreds of chattering, squeaking baby bats.

During birth a female bat grasps a perch with her thumbs, hangs right side up, and tucks her tail membrane between her legs to form a pouch. The baby bat emerges feet first. The pouch acts as a sort of safety net to prevent the baby from falling to the ground.

A Micro is usually quite helpless at birth. It is born naked and blind. Its ears are stuck close to its head, and it must cling very tightly to its mother. After she has licked her baby clean, the mother helps it to crawl up her belly to a nipple and suck her life-sustaining milk. A baby bat has curved milk teeth for clinging to

This female red bat at left has formed a pouch with her tail membrane to hold her babies. Red bats have a lot of brightly colored fur and are common in the eastern half of the United States. Bats are born without any fur. This Mexican free-tailed baby bat above is clinging to its mother's back. Free-tailed bats can be seen in the south and southwestern part of the United States.

its mother's nipples and well-developed thumbs and claws for grasping her fur.

For the first few days the baby may remain attached to its mother. At night, as she flies out of the roost to find food, it hangs on with all its might. Soon, though, the baby becomes too heavy to be carried. It must be left behind in the nursery to cling with its hooked toes to the wall or ceiling of the roost.

Sometimes the young drop from their perches. Unable to fly, they are not always strong enough to climb back up. The adults seem unable to help the young when they fall. Sometimes they hover around a baby bat as it lies on the ground, squeaking pitifully. But they soon fly away and the young bat eventually starves to death.

Occasionally female bats have been known to help their young. In Ceylon a baby bat that had become separated from its mother was picked up by a man and taken into his house. In the evening a female bat, perhaps attracted by the baby's squeaks, flew into the room. She suckled the young bat and flew off again with it clinging to her breast.

When the females return from their feeding flights early in the morning, they immediately suckle the young that have been left behind in the roost. Experts are divided on the question of whether female bats can actually recognize their own offspring. There may be hundreds of babies hanging in the nursery chambers, and some experts believe the mothers suckle the nearest youngster at hand.

The young grow quickly. Their eyes soon open and within a few weeks they are able to spread their wings and take their first flights. Now they must learn to catch and feed on insects.

FINDING THEIR WAY IN THE DARK

As twilight approaches, caves and other bat roosts start to come alive. At first only a few shadowy forms can be seen in the gloom as the early risers dart toward the exit holes to test the light. Then, as more and more bats awake, the air fills with the sound of squeaks and flapping wings. Sometimes the noise can be deafening. It has been compared to the sound of a train racing through a tunnel, and even to the sound of a jet engine.

As the bats fly out of the roost, they rise high in the air and head for a nearby lake or pond. Then they swoop down to the surface, scooping up water with their lower jaws before flying off in search of their first meal. By this time, woods, fields, gardens, parks, and beaches may all be covered with darkness. Yet somehow the bats manage to find their way at night. They not only avoid crashing into trees, houses, telegraph poles, and other obstacles, but they also find and catch hosts of flying insects. How do they do it?

Many people assume that bats rely to a large extent on sensitive vision to find their way in the dark, like owls and cats and other nighttime hunters. Cats and owls have large eyes that can gather all the available light, but they cannot see in total darkness. Micros, on the other hand, have very small eyes. Even so, they do not require any light at all in order to find their way. They can fly accurately through pitch-black caves.

How, then, do bats find their way?

The first pieces of the puzzle were put together by an Italian naturalist, Lazaro Spallanzani, in the eighteenth century. Spallanzani (1729–99) first became interested in the behavior of nocturnal animals when he was sixty-four years old. At that time he had a pet owl that was allowed to fly around his room. One winter night in 1793, as Spallanzani was working by candlelight, the owl flew too close to the flame, and it went out. The scientist was startled to hear the owl crashing into the walls and furniture in the dark. Why, Spallanzani wondered, was a nocturnal animal like an owl disoriented when it found itself in complete darkness? He decided to capture some bats, to find out if they reacted in the same way. He let the bats loose in his darkened room and they flew quite normally, without knocking into anything.

Spallanzani became even more curious. He decided to blind several bats to find out if they could find their way without any sight at all. The blinded bats flew perfectly, weaving around the obstacles in his room. The scientist then decided to find out if blinded bats were still able to catch insects and feed. He captured some bats from a bell tower nearby, blinded them, and returned them to their roost. A few days later he recovered four of the blinded bats at the tower. He dissected them; and found that their stomachs were full of insects.

Now thoroughly intrigued, Spallanzani set to work on further experiments. Eventually he and a fellow scientist, Charles Jurine, discovered that bats stumbled in the dark only when their ears and mouths were covered. "Can it then be," asked Spallanzani, "their ears rather than their eyes served to direct them in flight?"

Spallanzani died before his "bat problem," as it became known, could be solved. Most scientists of the day decided that bats simply avoided obstacles by their sense of touch. The real reason was not discovered until our own century.

ECHOLOCATION

In 1938 a young Harvard undergraduate, Donald R. Griffin, was experimenting with ringed bats in order to study their migration patterns. At that time he was familiar with the accepted view that bats avoided obstacles by their sense of touch. But he had also heard of a theory put forward by an English scientist, H. Hartridge, in 1920. Hartridge had suggested that bats might be able to avoid obstacles by sending out sound signals.

Friends encouraged Griffin to do some firsthand research on bat flight. He approached a Harvard professor, G. W. Pierce, who was doing pioneer research work on *ultrasonic* sounds — sounds that are so high-pitched they are beyond the range of human hearing. The professor's laboratory contained almost the only instruments in the world that were capable of detecting such sounds. He agreed to help Griffin with his research. When Griffin placed his cage of bats in front of the instruments, and adjusted the tuning dial, "a medley of raucous noises" came over the loudspeaker. The young student and Professor Pierce were the first people to learn that bats produce ultrasonic sounds.

We can hear the very loud sounds bats make when hundreds congregate. Because of Dr. Griffin's experiments we now know that bats also send out very high-pitched sounds that we cannot hear at all. These sounds usually range in frequency from 30,000 *cycles*, or vibrations, per second to 100,000 cycles per second. Humans only hear sounds in the frequency ranges below 20,000 cycles per second, although young children can sometimes hear sounds above this range. Bats have extremely good hearing. They are able to pick up the echoes of these sound signals as the sounds bounce off objects in their flight path, such as branches or flying insects. The time lag between the sounds and the returning echoes tells the bats how far away the objects are. This extraordinary way of avoiding obstacles and finding prey is known as **echolocation.**

Bats are not the only animals to use echolocation. Another unusual mammal, the whale, finds its way and its food in the depths of the oceans by sending out sound signals and picking up the returning echoes. Scientists also use echolocation devices. **Radar** works by echolocation and is used to detect objects, such as aircraft, in the air. And **sonar** is used to locate objects under-water. But a bat's built-in system of echolocation is more precise than any of those yet invented by humans. While radar can detect an object hundreds of miles away, the object has to be at least several yards wide. A bat can detect an insect only ⅓ inch long from 6 feet away.

NOSES, MOUTHS, AND EARS

When you look at bats close up, the first thing you notice about them is their strange-looking faces. The ears, noses, and mouths of each species look quite different. It almost seems as though someone had come along with modeling clay, punched out the weirdest shapes he could think of, then stuck them on at ran-

A rounded thin nose leaf in the shape of a horseshoe has given the greater horseshoe bat its name.

The spearlike tragus, or earlet, of this mouse-eared
bat can be easily seen at the base of the outer ear.
Unlike bats with nose leaves, this bat keeps its
mouth open while sending out high-pitched sounds.

dom. Bats have large, horn-shaped ears, lumpy, fleshy noses, and grooved and wrinkled mouths. These unusual shapes may look strange, but they all have a purpose. They are aids to more precise echolocation.

Some Micros send out their high-pitched sounds through their mouths. They keep their mouths open as they fly and purse their lips to beam the sounds forward. *Moustache bats* make a horn shape with their lips. Other Micros fly with their lips closed and send out sounds through their nostrils. These bats have folds of skin around their noses, shaped like spears and snouts and even horseshoes. These appendages are called **nose leaves** and vary in structure and shape from species to species. They also help to beam sound effectively.

Bats' ultrasonic sounds do not spread in all directions. They travel in an arc directly in front of their mouths and noses. Dr. Griffin once measured the strength, or intensity, of sound a few inches in front of a bat's mouth with special equipment. He found it was twenty times greater than the sound of a drill breaking up a city pavement! Perhaps it's just as well that we cannot hear the sounds bats make.

Bats need extremely sensitive hearing for echolocation. The sound signals they send out last only 1/1000 to 1/100 second. So, within a fraction of a second after they have sent out a deafening burst of sound, they must be able to pick up the returning echoes. The echoes may be 2,000 time fainter than the original pulse. Bats' ears are very large in proportion to the rest of their bodies and their hearing has become adapted to their special needs.

A bat's ears, like those of all mammals, have three parts, or chambers. There is an outer, a middle, and an inner ear. The outer ear is shaped to collect sounds. The sounds pass into the middle ear, where they vibrate on the eardrum. Then they pass into the inner ear where they stimulate nerve cells. The nerve cells send messages to the brain, which interprets them as sounds. A bat's ears are set farther apart from each other than in other mammals. This is very helpful to echolocation. Depending on which direction the echoes are traveling from, one ear will pick up the echoes slightly before the other ear. This time lag helps bats to judge distances and directions.

Many species of Micros have an earlet, called the **tragus,** that points up in front of the outer ear like a lance. It helps to channel the echo through the outer ear.

CATCHING INSECTS

If you have ever seen a bat wheeling and diving, swooping and somersaulting through the air, you already know that its flight pattern looks very wild. Yet every acrobatic movement a bat makes usually means it is chasing or catching an insect. If conditions are good, a bat may catch as many as fourteen insects a minute.

When it is cruising for food, a bat sends out between 5 and 20 sound pulses a second. As an insect is detected, the bat's sound pulses increase to as many as 200 a second. This is like an outboard motor opening up from slowest idling to full speed in less than a second.

At the moment of capture a bat throws its legs forward, so that its tail membrane forms a pouch between its legs. The insect is caught up in this pouch, then the bat quickly lowers its head to seize the insect with its sharp teeth. Sometimes bats use their wing tips to sweep insects into their tail pouches. Sometimes they simply catch them in their open mouths.

Yet how do bats tell the difference between the echoes they are receiving from insect prey and echoes they are also receiving from objects in their path, such as branches and leaves? The answer seems quite simple. Bats tested in a laboratory in which wires had been hung were subjected to severe noise from a loudspeaker. They flew in patterns that caused the noise from the loudspeaker and the echoes from the wires to reach their ears from different directions. In this way they were able to sort out the different noises, judge distances, and dodge the wires.

Bats detect insect echoes from a few inches to a few yards away. They receive echoes from large objects over greater distances, but probably cannot detect any object that is more than half a mile away. This is one of the reasons that bats are believed to rely on vision when they migrate.

ANSWERING BACK

Bats eat many kinds of insects including flies, winged ants, termites, locusts, beetles, mosquitoes, crickets, and dragonflies. But night-flying moths seem to be their favorite prey. Yet bats are not always successful in capturing moths. Some kinds of moths have developed a weapon to aid them in their battle for survival. They can actually hear the ultrasonic pulses sent out by bats.

Scientists have discovered that moths have "ears" along the sides of their bodies which are not only sensitive to the frequency range most commonly used by bats, but also to frequencies far above it. As soon as they hear a bat approaching, some moths fly away, spiraling through the air or dropping to the ground before the bat can catch up. While they do not always escape, the moths have an advantage. Because they can hear ultrasonic sounds over greater distances than bats can hear the returning echoes, they get a head start in the chase.

Lately scientists have discovered that some night-flying moths are not only able to hear bats' ultrasonic sounds but are also able to send out ultrasonics of their own. By turning the tables in this manner, they are able to frighten bats away with their own sounds. The sounds are thought to act as warnings that the moths are distasteful, in much the same way that the bright colors of wasps warn birds that they are poisonous and not worth catching.

THE FISHING BATS

Not all Micros feed on insects. A few species have more exotic tastes. But whatever their diets, all Micros use echolocation to guide them in their hunt for food. The insect eaters send out the most intense sounds, though. Other bats "whisper" in comparison.

One of the most unusual bat diets is fish. Fish-eating bats are closely related to insect-eating bats. Some of the insect-eaters have been seen scooping up bugs from the surface of rivers with their jaws. The ability to catch fish may have developed from this habit.

The best-known fishing bat is found in Mexico and South America. Its scientific name is *Noctilio leporinus*. Large and powerful, with a wingspan of nearly ` feet, *Noctilio* flies low over lakes, rivers, and even oceans, plucking fish from the water with its strong hooked claws. While it usually leaves its roost at dusk to feed, on occasion it has been seen feeding beside pelicans in broad daylight, catching fish as they rose to the surface in an effort to flee from the diving birds.

Many insect-eating bats like moths. This serotine bat looks very much like its close relative the big brown bat, or house bat. The house bat is the most familiar of all species in the United States.

CARNIVORES
AND CANNIBALS

Some of the largest species of Micros are *carnivores*, or flesh eaters. They hunt other animals for food. Mice, birds, frogs, and even nocturnal lizards may all be on their menus. Sometimes the carnivorous bats are cannibals, too; they eat smaller bats as well as other fare.

Flesh-eating bats are found in Asia, South America, and Australia. The Asian species are known as *false vampire bats* and have a wingspan of around 2 feet. They do not lap blood like the true vampires, but they do eat small animals and other bats. Their cannibalistic habits were first discovered in 1842 by a British naturalist, Edward Blyth, while he was on a visit to India.

One evening a false vampire flew into his room. Blyth quickly closed the door so it could not escape. As he turned, he noticed that the bat had dropped something. Thinking it was a baby bat, Blyth stooped to pick it up. To his amazement he found it was a small bat of another species which had a bleeding wound behind its ear. That night Blyth placed both bats together in a cage. But as soon as it saw the smaller bat, the false vampire "fastened on it with the ferocity of a tiger." Within a short time it devoured the smaller bat, leaving only its head and part of its wings.

Among South American carnivorous bats the most well known is the *spear-nosed bat*, a fierce-looking creature with sharp, pointed teeth and a wingspread of 2½ feet. A scientist who managed to catch one kept it in a laboratory in Panama for more than five months in order to study its feeding habits. During its period of captivity the bat ate three birds, twenty-five house mice, thirteen bats, and "a considerable ration of banana." When tackling prey, the bat would seize it by the neck, then bite through its skull to kill it. Starting with the head, it would then slowly devour the body, leaving only the hind end and tail. If it was really hungry, the bat would gobble up every inch of its victim.

THE VEGETARIANS

A few Micros eat only vegetarian food. Known as *leaf-nosed bats*, they live mainly in tropical parts of South America. Occasionally some venture into the southernmost parts of the United States.

Leaf-nosed bats feed on fruit and the pollen and nectar of flowering plants. Because their food is available all year round, they do not need to migrate or hibernate. Still they do live quite nomadic lives, traveling from place to place to find the best food sources.

Bananas and plantains are the favorite food of leaf-nosed bats. Farmers have found that they must cut bananas while they are still green. Otherwise their crops will be ruined by hordes of bats that eat the soft ripe fruits and leave the skins dangling from the trees. A scientist once caught sixty bats in a matter of minutes simply by hanging a bunch of ripe bananas in his room as bait.

In the West Indies, some bats carry palm nuts back to their roosts so that they can feed unhurriedly on the soft fruit inside. Sometimes the floors of their caves become so strewn with nuts that some of the seeds germinate and send up white shoots to a height of 2 or 3 feet before they die from lack of sunlight.

Some of the leaf-nosed bats feed only on pollen and nectar. They have long, narrow tongues with stiff hairs at the tip which form a sort of brush. They lap up the nectar with this "brush" and

serve as *pollinators* (carriers of pollen) as they go from flower to flower. Pollen and nectar feeding habits may originally have developed from insect-eating habits. When grabbing an insect from a flower, a bat may also have gotten a taste of the sweet nectar and nutritious pollen and acquired a liking for it.

THE VAMPIRES

Of all the Micros none have more extraordinary feeding habits than the vampires. They live by piercing the skins of other animals with their teeth, then lapping up their blood. A single vampire may drink fifteen pints of blood a year.

There are three different kinds of vampire bats. They all live in tropical parts of Central and South America and are found nowhere else in the world. The most common vampire is a species known as *Desmodus*. Though it has a frightening reputation, *Desmodus* is actually not much bigger than a sparrow. It weighs less than two ounces. Brownish in color, it has small, pointed ears, a tiny wrinkled nose leaf, and a wingspan of 10-15 inches. Only the shape of its mouth suggests its blood-drinking habit — its lower lip is deeply grooved. The groove acts like a tube, or a drinking straw, to draw up blood.

Vampires roost in hollow trees or caves, often sharing their homes with other species of bats. They do not attack their roost-

**A South American leaf-nosed bat.
This greater Artibeus fruit bat
has a well-developed tragus in
addition to a prominent nose leaf.**

mates. They prefer larger animals — poultry, sheep, cattle, horses, goats, pigs, dogs, and people. In the late evening, when animals have bedded down for the night and human beings are sleeping, vampires emerge from their roosts to seek food. They are attracted by an animal's body heat and smell, and they also use echolocation to hunt down their victims.

Vampires are very stealthy when they hunt. They have soft pads on their wrist joints and often move cautiously on the ground instead of flying. In this way they do not wake their intended victims and risk being kicked by a heavy hoof or lashed by a strong tail. Landing gently on an animal, a vampire first seeks an exposed area of skin: the face, nose, ears, neck, lips, feet, or toes. Then it makes a small cut with its sharp, curved teeth, slices away a tiny piece of skin, and starts to lap the blood. Its saliva contains a substance that stops the blood from clotting so it flows easily. Most victims, including human beings, continue sleeping during an attack and are unaware they are providing a vampire with a blood meal. When they wake in the morning, a small wound may be the only sign they have been bitten.

Fortunately for people who live in South America, vampires can be kept away with mosquito nets. But human beings are usually the vampires' last choice anyway. They seem to prefer the blood of cattle to any other animal. This straightforward diet means that vampires can be kept quite easily in zoos. The Bronx Zoo in New York City has four vampire bats and receives a regular supply of blood from a slaughterhouse to feed them. The blood is kept in a deep-freeze, then thawed as it is needed. The vampires lap up about two-thirds of an ounce of blood each per day from special containers.

In the wild, blood-drinking habits become more destructive.

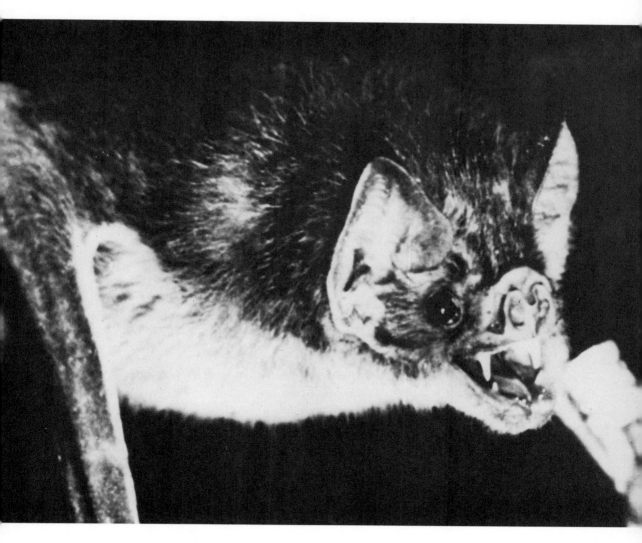

A vampire bat has sharp, hooked teeth for biting and specially adapted knee joints that allow it to move around on the ground when approaching its victims.

A moderate-sized colony containing 100 vampires roosting together in a cave would need some 186 gallons of blood a year. This is the equivalent of the blood contained in 25 cows. Vampires feed over a fairly small range, probably only a few square miles around their roost. This means that all the blood has to come from one fairly small area. Poultry, birds, and other small animals may be drained of their life-blood in a single night. Larger animals, such as cows, rarely die of blood loss but they may be seriously weakened if they are continually attacked. Farmers have tried different methods to protect their cattle, but none is entirely successful. Sometimes cattle farmers find they just have to accept their losses.

RABIES

Many vampires carry a disease known as rabies. When rabies-infected (rabid) bats bite other animals, the disease virus is often passed on in their saliva.

Rabies affects the central nervous system. There is usually a "furious" stage of the disease, followed by paralysis and death.

The little brown bat is very common in the northern United States. Ranging in color from pale tan to dark brown, it may be found roosting in attics in the summertime. In winter it hibernates in caves and mines.

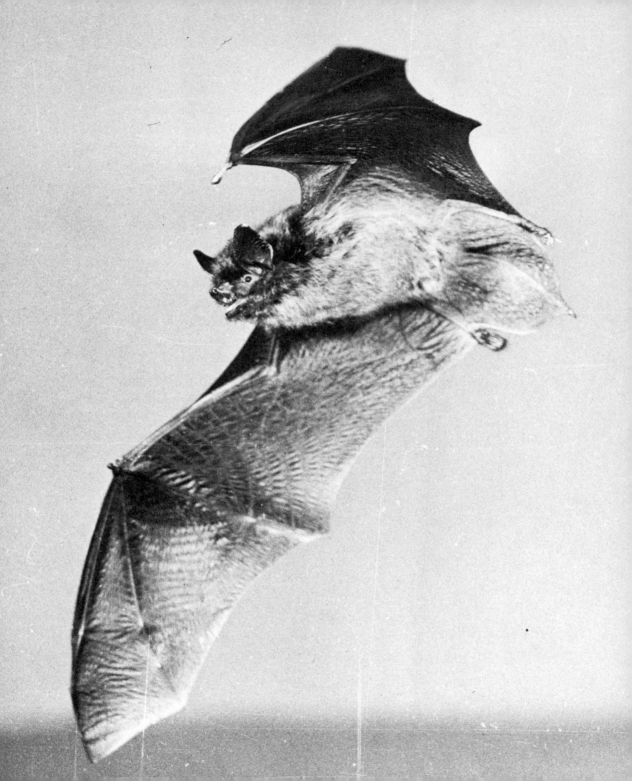

One of the most horrifying symptoms in human beings is a hysterical fear of water. People who get rabies may find swallowing so painful that the mere sight of a glass of water sends them into fits of terror. And they may become extremely aggressive in their behavior. Animals with rabies often attack other animals, or human beings who are unfortunate enough to cross their path.

Until recently vampires were the only species of bat known to carry rabies. Then in 1953 three people in different areas of the United States — Texas, Pennsylvania, and Florida — were bitten by rabid Micros. Since that time forty-eight of the fifty states have reported the presence of rabid bats and six people have died from bat-transmitted rabies.

Despite these unfortunate deaths, bat-transmitted rabies is far less of a hazard in the United States than in Latin America. The tropical vampire bats of Central and South America have to bite in order to feed. But the insect-eating bats of the United States do not normally come in contact with people at all. And if they do, their teeth are generally not sharp enough to penetrate human skin. Still, it is dangerous to pick up bats, disturb them in their roosts, or enter bat caves. Though Micros do not usually bite human beings, they may do so if they are handled, or if they are suffering from the "furious" stage of rabies. Anyone who is bitten by a bat should immediately wash the wound thoroughly and seek medical advice at once.

PREVENTING RABIES

Rabies is one of the world's oldest-known diseases. All warm-blooded animals can become infected with it and pass it on. Rabies has been recorded in every country in the world, except

Australia, though careful control measures keep many areas completely free of the disease.

Outside Latin America, dogs are the animals most likely to infect human beings. Dogs, in turn, catch the disease from infected wild animals that they come in contact with. In the United States, skunks, foxes, and coyotes are the most common carriers of infection. Rabies is usually transmitted from animal to animal by biting.

Up until the last century there were no preventive measures that could be taken by people bitten by rabid animals. The wounds were cauterized (burned) with a red-hot iron by the local blacksmith, and the victim just had to hope the disease would not appear. Then in 1881 the French scientist Louis Pasteur began to experiment with antirabies **vaccines.** He injected healthy rabbits with infected tissue from rabid animals. After many years of experiments, he was able to obtain a form of the virus that could be used as a vaccine.

Since that time many millions of people who have been exposed to rabies have been effectively treated with vaccinations. They are injected with a weakened strain of the virus. The body then naturally forms antibodies, substances that fight off the disease. The incubation period of rabies — the time it takes for first symptoms to appear — is normally quite long. It takes about three to six weeks or longer for human beings, and ten days to six months for other animals. The body is therefore able to build up enough antibodies to combat the weakened virus before the disease has time to develop. Once someone has built up antibodies against a disease, he or she is protected from catching that disease for a considerable period of time.

For highly susceptible people there is some risk that the

weakened virus in the vaccine will bring on the disease. It is for this reason that vaccinations are generally given to people only *after* exposure to the disease. However, a vaccination must be given *immediately* after contact. Once rabies has set in, there is no known cure. Cattle and other livestock may be given pre-exposure vaccinations with much greater safety. Where rabies is common, animals are given antirabies shots as a matter of routine.

Most countries have strict laws designed to prevent the spread of rabies. No bats may be imported into the United States at all except for special scientific purposes. Dogs that have not been vaccinated against rabies at least a month before entry must be confined for a period of 30 days. Each state has centers where laboratory tests can be performed on animals suspected of having rabies. Rabid animals should be destroyed and taken to the nearest test center for examination. These precautions make rabies much less of a threat in the United States today than in earlier times.

BATS IN THE BELFRY

For hundreds of years, bats have been associated with madness. Even today many people tap their heads knowingly when someone behaves in a peculiar way and use the words "bats in the belfry" or "batty" as an explanation.

This association may have developed from the spread of bat-transmitted rabies in ancient times. The word *rabies* comes from the Latin word *rabidus,* meaning "raving." The connection between the appearance of bats suffering from the "furious" stage of rabies and the sudden change in the behavior of a diseased animal or person would not have been hard to make.

It is refreshing to learn that there is one country in the world where bats are very definitely not associated with madness, or with anything unpleasant at all. That country is China. In Chinese the word for bat is *fu*, which also happens to be the name of the character meaning "happiness." If a Chinese person gives you a present bearing the symbol of a bat, it means that he or she is wishing you the greatest fortune of all — good luck.

WHAT ABOUT HAIR?

One of the most widely held superstitions about bats is that they are attracted to hair. Many people believe that a bat will fly around a woman's head and become so entangled in her hair that the two can only be parted with a pair of scissors. The victims are generally supposed to be women because women usually have longer hair and more elaborate hairstyles. When you consider that bats can avoid fine wires and other obstacles by echolocation, the whole idea seems very unlikely. Still, people continue to believe that bats have a natural liking for women's hair.

Britain's Lord Cranbrook, an enthusiastic naturalist, decided to conduct his own research to put this superstition to rest for once and for all. His first experiments were conducted with four differen species of bats and two eighteen-year-old young women with blond hair. One of them had fairly short, curly hair, and the other had long, wavy hair that she wore in a bun.

"Each species was placed in turn upon the volunteer's head," reports Lord Cranbrook. "Each walked about without becoming entangled in any way, and finally took flight without any difficulty."

Later, Lord Cranbrook decided to try the same bat-in-hair experiment with a middle-aged brunette, in case hair color or age affected bat behavior in any way. The woman in question was first strengthened for the experiment with a glass of wine. Then Lord Cranbrook lifted up her hair, placed a bat on it, and covered the bat with the top layer. Even so, the bat had no trouble getting out from underneath.

Says Lord Cranbrook of his female volunteers, "I should like to be able to record the names of these martyrs to science, but they prefer to remain anonymous."

THE TROPICAL MEGAS

The time was June 1770. The setting was a beach in northern Australia, where Captain James Cook's ship *The Endeavour* was at anchor. The crew was repairing the ship's hull and the sound of mallets hammered through the air. Suddenly there was a shout. A seaman who had wandered off into the bush to explore burst through the trees onto the beach, waving his arms wildly and calling to the crew. The sailor told his startled companions of an enormous animal he had just seen. It had wings, he said, was about the size of a gallon keg, and looked just like the devil. A scouting party set off into the bush to search for the creature.

And that, so the story goes, is how the *flying fox*, the largest species of bat in the world, was first discovered by Europeans.

Flying foxes, so-called because their faces look so much like like those of foxes and dogs, belong to the second suborder of bats: the Megachiroptera, or larger bats. One flying fox in the collection of the American Museum of Natural History, in New York City, has a wingspan of just over 5 feet, 4 inches, about the length of a bathtub. One 5-foot, 7-inch flying fox has been caught, and some are believed to have a wingspan of nearly 6 feet.

Not all the bats that belong to the suborder Megachiroptera are as large as flying foxes, but they are generally larger than Micros. Most are much more appealing to look at, too. This is because they do not use echolocation to find food and so have no need of wrinkled nose leaves or spearlike ears.

Megas are strictly vegetarian feeders and are found only in tropical parts of Australia, Africa, and Asia, where fruit grows or flowers blossom all year round.

SQUABBLES AT DAWN

Flying foxes and nearly all the other Megas spend their lives in the open. They hang from the branches of trees during the day and search for food in the cool of the evening. Generally they have brighter-colored fur than the Micros, in rich shades of chestnut or mahogany. Often they have white markings on their heads and bodies, too. The markings help to break up the general outlines of their bodies so they are harder to spot among branches and leaves. This camouflage, or disguise, probably helps to hide them from enemies.

Noisy, sociable creatures, Megas usually roost together in treetops in large colonies, or camps. Sometimes so many bats gather together that the branches bend down under their weight. Their collective shrieks and calls can be heard over a mile away.

This happy-looking creature is an Egyptian fruit bat, also known as a dog-faced bat.

The greatest commotion occurs at dawn as the bats return from feeding trips. The early arrivals settle down on the topmost branches of the trees. Then as more and more bats arrive, squabbles break out as each one tries to find enough room to roost comfortably. Bickering and screeching and flapping their wings, like angry birds, the bats eventually space themselves out so each has enough room.

Generally it is midmorning before the quarrels finally subside. Then the bats doze, each one hanging upside down by its feet. In this position, the bat tucks its head against its breast and folds its wings over its face and body as a shield against the glare of the sun. Sometimes, during intense heat, long rows of Megas may fan themselves with one or other lazy, flapping wing.

As darkness falls, the bats wake and prepare for another night's feeding. Now there is less noise as they busy themselves by smoothing their fur with their claws and licking their bodies and wings clean. Usually they leave the roost silently in small groups.

FEEDING HABITS

The vast majority of Megas feed on fruit. Bananas, figs, apples, breadfruit, mangoes, plantains, papaws, peaches, avocados, berries, guavas, and small, juicy coconuts are all devoured by Megas. The bats tear at the husks with their long, sharp canine teeth, then crush and grind the fruit with their flat-topped molars. Usually they spit out the fleshy pulp and seeds and swallow only the sweet juice.

Only one group of fruit eaters uses echolocation. They are called *rousettus bats* and live in Africa and southern Asia. They make clicking sounds with their tongues and are the only Megas that are able to take advantage of dark caves as roosting sites.

All the other Megas find their food in the dark by using their senses of sight and smell. Their eyes are large and bright, like the gleaming buttons in the fur of teddy bears. Although they cannot find their way in complete darkness, Megas can see in very dim light, because the retina of their eyes has a larger surface area for picking up light than any other mammal's. Megas probably have much better vision than other nocturnal animals, too, such as owls and cats.

Megas also use their acute sense of smell to find food. Ripe fruit gives off a powerful odor and an orchard may attract thousands of bats. Even bowls of fruit lying on tables in people's homes may attract passing bats.

A few of the smaller Megas feed on nectar and pollen. They are found mostly in Africa. Like some of the vegetarian Micros, they have slender tongues with brushlike hairs at the tip for lapping up their food. Because they dart from tree to tree, these bats also act as pollinators.

Some trees seem to be specially adapted in order to attract bats and so ensure their help in pollination. They send out a strong odor and have large flowers that open only at night. When a bat inserts its head and shoulders into a blossom to feed on the nectar, the pollen clings to its fur, then scatters as it moves on to the next flower.

BATS IN CAPTIVITY

Megas are the bats most usually found in zoos. They are better suited to life in captivity than Micros. This is because their fruit-eating habits make them much easier to feed. Micros sometimes

Fruit bats can be affectionate and playful.
Dr. Cherrie Bramwell and her pet bat
Paul clearly enjoy each other's company.

consume hundreds of insects a day, and over a long period of captivity vast quantities of insects would be needed to feed just a few insectivorous bats. Although Micros have sometimes been kept by people as pets, they cannot adapt to family life as dogs or cats can. Micros are not "intelligent" in the normal sense of the word. For instance, a Micro may bite the hand that feeds it, or even refuse to eat at all for some time. As it becomes tamer, it may appear to recognize its "owner" and learn to accept food offered from forceps or fingers. But a Micro will rarely learn to eat food from a dish. And, after all, why should it? It is used to flying and using echolocation to find food. Not surprisingly, most pet Micros sicken and die within a few months. It is much kinder to let a Micro live the life that nature intended for it.

People have been known to keep Megas as pets. When Dr. Cherrie Bramwell, of England, was studying for her doctorate she kept a bat called Paul in her apartment for two years in order to study his habits. When she first bought Paul from a pet shop, he was frightened and nervous. Although still a baby, measuring only 7 inches from foot to nose, he had lost most of his fur.

Dr. Bramwell fed him by hand for three months, on bananas, apples, and peaches. She kept him warm and comfortable during the day in an old parrot cage. The door of the cage was removed, so Paul was free to fly around the room. Now, six years later, Paul is a healthy adult bat measuring 14 inches from foot to nose and with a wingspan of 5 feet.

Paul quickly became tame under Dr. Bramwell's constant care. "It was like having a little dog," she says. "He would greet me by flopping across the floor, then climbing up to his favorite position around my neck." Clasping Dr. Bramwell's neck, Paul's back would hang down the front of her body. "When I went out with Paul, people thought I was wearing a fur scarf. That is, until he suddenly poked his head out of my coat. Then he looked like a little chihuahua." Paul never tried to fly away when Dr. Bramwell took him outdoors, but she used to hang on to one of his ankles just in case.

Dr. Bramwell believes that Megas are intelligent creatures. They have a "knowing" look in their eyes, she says, and appear to use their sense of smell to identify objects. "Paul would make a purry, snuffly noise and rub noses with me. It was by using his sense of smell in this way that he was able to recognize me."

Each day Paul would take a small cup of tea with Dr. Bramwell, from his own special cup. He also developed quite a liking for alcohol. "If I was drinking a sherry or a glass of mulled wine, he would flip out a claw and pull the glass towards his mouth."

Paul now lives at the London Zoo, but Dr. Bramwell still visits him. Sometimes she even takes him back to her home for a "vacation."

BALANCING NUMBERS

No one can deny that there are a few "black sheep" among the various bat families. In Latin America the vampire bats may spell death for numbers of human beings and cattle each year. In Australia and other tropical areas the Megas sometimes cause considerable damage to fruit crops.

Yet bats, like all other animals, have a role to play in nature. Micros act mainly as a check on the dense population of insects. Insects often transmit diseases to humans and other animals, and cause damage to crops and foodstuffs. A survey in Texas has shown that free-tailed bats alone consume some 6,600 tons of insects in the area each year.

And while Megas eat quantities of fruit, many species also carry seeds or pollen so that new crops flourish. Megas also serve as a basic food supply for protein-starved people in tropical parts of the world. To us, bats may not sound appetizing, but the taste of their roasted flesh has been compared to that of veal, pork, and chicken.

Bats do not have everything their own way, of course. They also have enemies, to limit their population growth. Great horned owls and barn owls sometimes make their homes near cave entrances and attack bats as they leave their roosts at night to feed. Other predatory birds, such as hawks, falcons, and kites, also feed on bats. Flesh-eating carnivores such as raccoons, bobcats, skunks, and opossums also find bats a tasty dish. They may wander into caves and feast upon baby bats that have fallen to the ground. In tropical areas Megas may be eaten by snakes and eagles. And sometimes, as they swoop down to rivers and lakes to drink, they are snatched up in the jaws of crocodiles.

Human beings are also often enemies of bats. It is obvious that bats carrying rabies must be destroyed if they are roosting near people's homes. But many harmless bats are also killed off each year through ignorance and superstition. It is only in the last decade or so that people have begun to realize that by recklessly killing wildlife they also disrupt natural food chains and upset the balance of nature.

Some nations, such as Great Britain, have passed laws designed to protect and conserve bats in their natural habitats. In this way, they may play their rightful and valuable role in nature — not as the mysterious winged devils of myth, but as wonderfully adapted flying mammals.

BIBLIOGRAPHY

Allen, Glover Morrill. *Bats*. New York: Dover Publications, 1962.

Barbour, Roger W., and Davis, Wayne H. *Bats of America*. Lexington: University of Kentucky Press, 1969.

Burton, Robert. *Animal Senses*. Devon, England: David & Charles, 1970.

Davis, John W.; Karstad, Lars H.; and Trainer, Daniel O., eds. *Infectious Diseases of Wild Mammals*. Ames: Iowa State University Press, 1970.

Griffin, Donald R. *Listening in the Dark*. New Haven, Conn.: Yale University Press, 1958.

Griffin, Donald R. "Bats: Animal Sonar Experts." *Animal Kingdom*. June, 1969.

Nicolle, Jacques. *Louis Pasteur: A Master of Scientific Enquiry*. London: Hutchinson, 1961.

Novick, A. "Echolocation in Bats." *Natural History*. March, 1970.

Peterson, Russell. *Silently, By Night*. London: Longmans, 1966.

Pye, David. *Bats*. London: Bodley Head, 1968.

Racey, P. A. *Small Mammals, 1: Bats*. London: Granada Publishing, 1973.

Simon, Seymour. *Life in the Dark*. New York: Franklin Watts, 1974.

Stoker, Bram. *Dracula*. London: Rider & Co., 1947. Originally published 1897.

Wimsatt, William A., ed. *Biology of Bats*. Vols. 1 & 2. New York and London: Academic Press, 1970.

INDEX

ABOUT THE AUTHOR

Valerie Pitt was born and educated in England. She has worked as a reporter and writer for several English newspapers and magazines and has written some thirty-five books for young readers, many of which have been published by Franklin Watts. She is the author of four natural history books in the new A Closer Look At picture book series. In addition, she is co-author, with Helen Hoke, of three other First Books: *Fleas, Owls,* and *Whales.* Valerie Pitt is currently living in London.